All About Walruses

ALL ABOUT ANIMALS IN THE SNOW

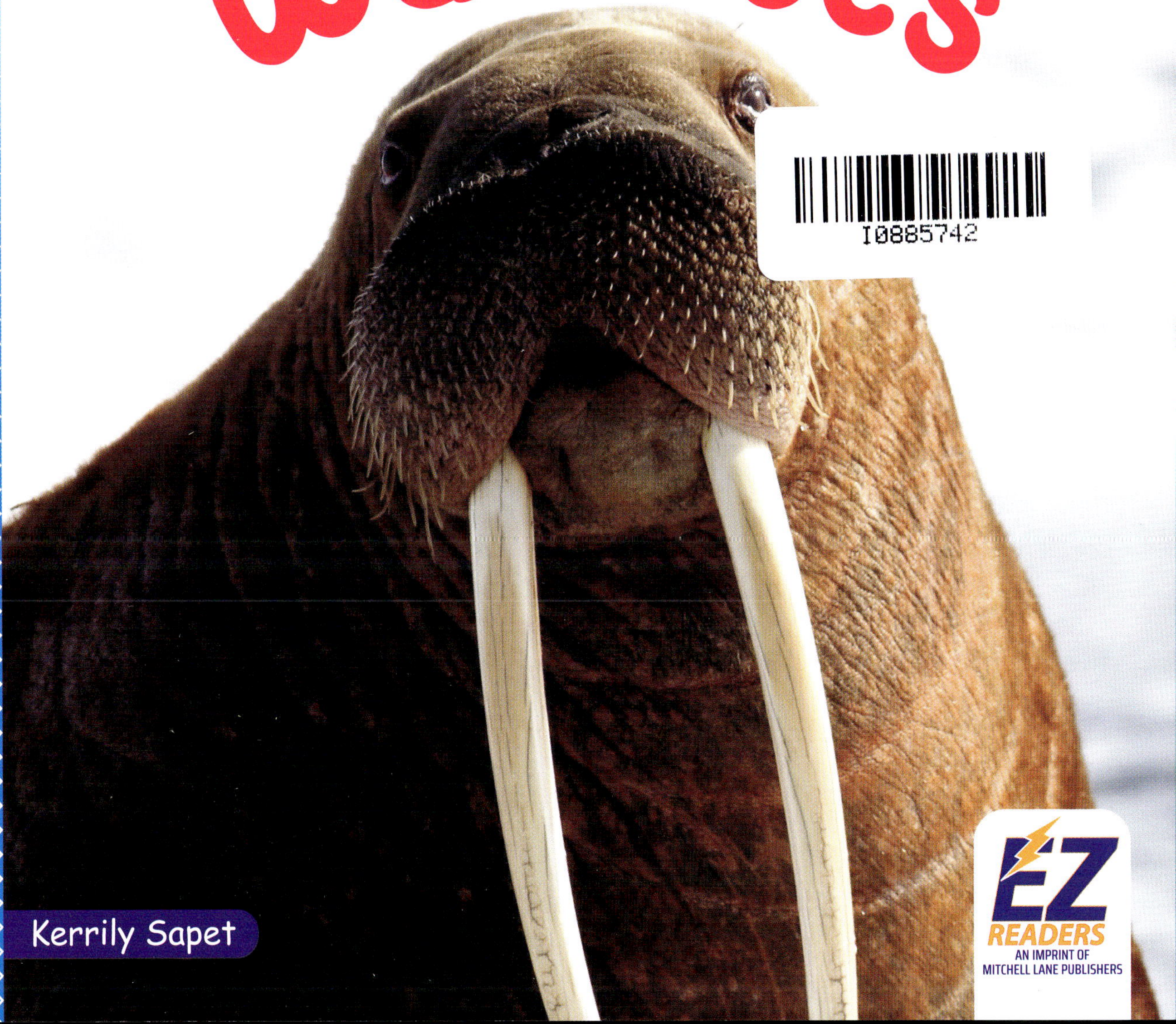

Kerrily Sapet

EZ READERS
AN IMPRINT OF MITCHELL LANE PUBLISHERS

CREATING YOUNG NONFICTION READERS

EZ Readers offer nonfiction for beginning readers in PreK through first grade, using simple language, clear illustrations, and engaging facts to build vocabulary and confidence.

TIPS FOR READING NONFICTION WITH BEGINNING READERS

Talk about Nonfiction

Begin by explaining that nonfiction books give us information that is true. The book will be organized around a specific topic or idea, and we may learn new facts through reading.

Look at the Parts

Most nonfiction books have helpful features. Our *EZ Readers* include color photographs and graphic aids, a table of contents, a glossary, and an index. Share the purpose of these features with your reader.

Color Photos and Graphic Aids

A lot of information can be found by "reading" photos, charts, maps, and other graphic aids found within nonfiction texts. Help your reader learn more about the different ways information can be displayed.

Table of Contents

Located at the front of the book, this list shows the big ideas within the text and the page numbers where they can be found.

Glossary

Located at the back of the book, the glossary defines key words and phrases that are related to the topic. These words and phrases can be found in the text in colored type.

Index

Located at the back of the book, an index is an alphabetical list of topics and the page numbers where they can be found.

With a little help and guidance about reading nonfiction, you can feel good about introducing a young reader to the world of *EZ Readers* nonfiction books.

EZ Readers is an imprint of:

Mitchell Lane
PUBLISHERS

2001 SW 31st Avenue
Hallandale, FL 33009
mitchelllanepub.com

First Edition, 2026.

Author: Kerrily Sapet
Editor: Morgan Brody

ISBN 979-8-89260-853-4 (library binding)
ISBN 979-8-90145-046-8 (paperback)
ISBN 979-8-89260-950-0 (ebook)

LC record available at https://lccn.loc.gov/2025950878

Photo credits: Adobe, Pixasquare, cover, 1, 2, 3, 4, 8, 12, 15, 19, 21, 22, 23, 24; Adobe, Tukinoto, cover, 1; Shutterstock, tryton2011, cover, 1; Vecteezy, Md. Shamim Akhtar, 3, 9, 10, 14, 18; Shutterstock, Irina WS, 5; Shutterstock, foto.t-kress.de, 6–7; Shutterstock, Aleksei Verhovski, 8, 22; Shutterstock, Adiyanto_123, 10–11; Shutterstock, theoldman, 12–13, 22; Shutterstock, Wirestock Creators, 12–13; Dreamstime, Binar Sariono, 14; Shutterstock, Mat Rowley, 16, 22; Shutterstock, Jonas Aleksander Larsen, 18, 22; Shutterstock, Lasse Johansson, 20; Shutterstock, woopics, 21; Shutterstock, grayjay, 22; Shutterstock, BlueRingMedia, 22; Wikimedia Commons, Alicia L. Bruzos and Seila Díaz Costas, 22

Table of Contents

Meeting An Arctic Animal

Imagine stepping outside in winter. The wind blasts your face. Your boots sink into the snow. Your coat is warm.

You see a huge animal moving slowly across the ice. It's brownish-pink, the color of cinnamon. It has two white **tusks**. A walrus! It's the size of a small car. Walruses live in the **Arctic**—one of the coldest places on Earth.

Walrus Watching

The walrus has wrinkly skin and **flippers**. Its face is covered in **whiskers**. Its tusks are longer than baseball bats. The walrus has a layer of fat called **blubber** to keep it warm.

WALRUS WOW!

Walruses have about 700 whiskers. Some whiskers are as long as spaghetti noodles.

WALRUS WOW!

Walruses are fast swimmers and can hold their breath for 10 minutes.

You see more walruses. One walrus is pulling its body out of the icy water using its tusks. Another walrus is smashing a hole in the ice with its tusks. It's making a breathing hole for swimming walruses.

The walruses are noisy! They grunt, bark, and whistle. They make sounds to **communicate** with each other.

WALRUS WOW!

A walrus can eat 3,000 clams in one feeding—enough to fill three refrigerators.

Looking for Food

One walrus dives underwater. It uses its whiskers to feel around the ocean floor. It finds a **clam**. The walrus sucks the soft part out of the clam. Walruses also eat snails and soft sea animals.

Where Do Walruses Live?

You see hundreds of walruses. They huddle together onshore like a pile of enormous puppies. A group of walruses is called a **haulout**.

Arctic Ocean
Asia
Europe
Atlantic Ocean
Africa
Pacific Ocean
South merica
Indian Ocean
Australia
KEY
Walrus habitat

WALRUS WOW!

Calves drink their mothers' milk. The milk is thick like butter.

Walrus Families and the Future

You see a baby! A baby walrus is called a **calf**. Calves are the size of large dogs. They ride on their mothers' backs in the water.

Walruses can live for 40 years. They need the ice on Earth to survive. Someday you might see a real walrus.

Parts of a Walrus

Ears

Walruses have small holes for ears. They can hear sounds up to a mile away. They listen for noises on land and while they are swimming.

Whiskers

Walruses have sensitive whiskers. Their whiskers help them detect food at the bottom of the ocean.

Tusk

Walruses have two long tusks. They use their tusks like ski poles to walk, pull themselves out of the water, and punch holes in the ice.

Skin

Walruses have thick, tough skin for protection. Their skin is 30 times thicker than a person's skin.

Flippers

Walruses have two front and two back flippers. Their flippers help them swim and walk on the slippery ice.

Glossary

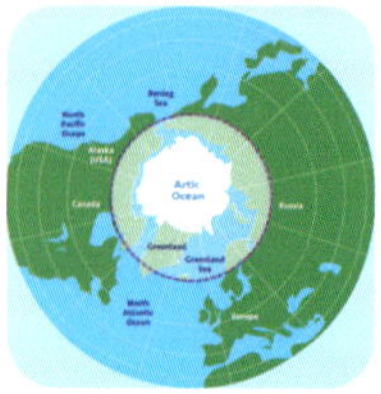

Arctic (ARK-tik) a very cold place near the top of the Earth where there is lots of ice and snow

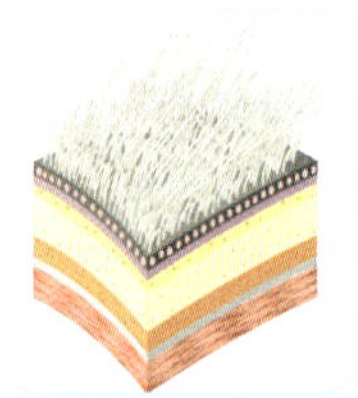

blubber (bluhb-er) a layer of fat under an animal's skin that keeps it warm

calf (kaf) a baby walrus

clam (klam) an ocean animal with a soft body inside a shell that closes tightly

communicate (kuh-myoon-i-kayt) to share ideas or feelings by making sounds or movements

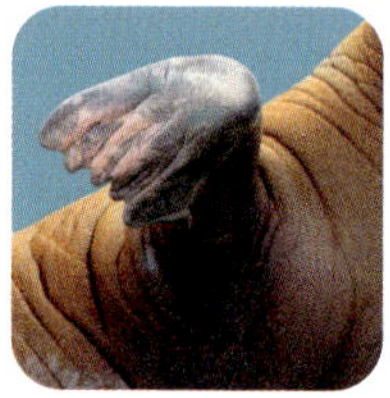

flippers (FLIP-erz) flat, paddle-shaped body parts that help animals swim

haulout (hawl-owt) a group of walruses

tusk (tuhsk) a long, pointed tooth that sticks out of some animal's mouths

whiskers (WISS-kerz) stiff hairs on an animal's face that help it feel and find things

Quiz

1. Do walruses live in lakes?

A. Yes B. No

2. Do walruses have tusks?

A. Yes B. No

3. Do walruses eat plants?

A. Yes B. No

4. Are walrus babies called a calf?

A. Yes B. No

ANSWER KEY — DO NOT PEEK!

ANSWER KEY:

1. No
2. Yes
3. No
4. Yes

Further Reading

Downs, Kieran. *Polar Bear vs. Walrus.* Bloomington, MN: Bellwether, 2021.

Lawler, Janet. *Walrus Song.* London, England: Walker Books, 2021.

Maloney, Brenda. *Arctic.* New York, NY: Scholastic, 2024.

On the Internet

Walruses

https://kids.nationalgeographic.com/animals/mammals/facts/walrus

Learn more and watch a video about walruses..

Walruses

https://www.pdza.org/the-walrus-boys/

Meet the walruses living at the Point Defiance Zoo & Aquarium.

Walrus Sounds

https://www.pdza.org/animals/rocky-shores/walrus/

Listen to the sounds walruses make.

Index

About the Author

Kerrily Sapet has written more than 40 books for kids. She lives near Chicago with her family. She likes snow and cold weather, just like walruses do! Sapet wrote this book to learn more about walruses. She has never seen a walrus at a zoo or in the wild. She hopes to see one someday.

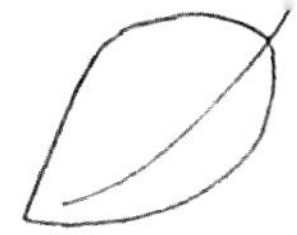

handmade
with love

handmade
with love

handmade
with love

handmade
with love

handmade
with love

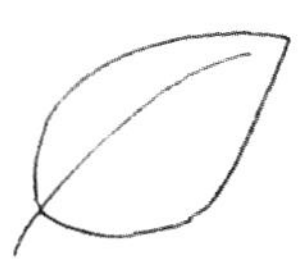

handmade
with love

handmade
with love

handmade
with love

handmade
with love

handmade
with love

handmade
with love

handmade
with love

handmade
with love

handmade with love

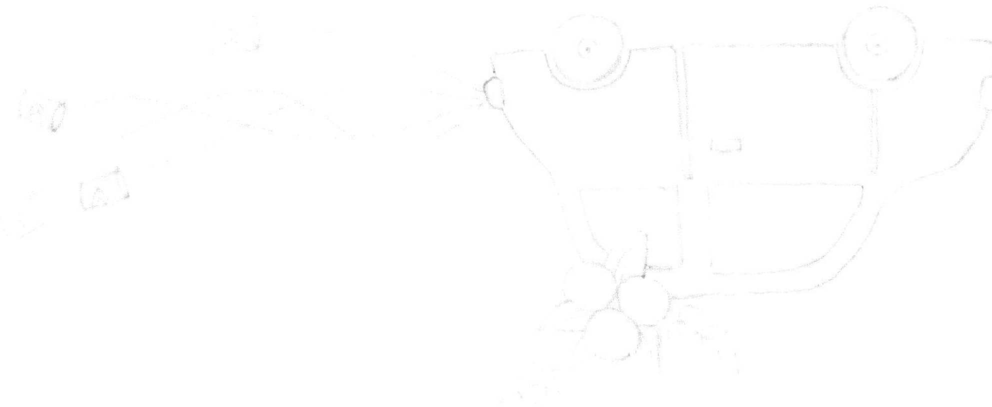

handmade
with love